IN THE YEAR OF THE TIGER

written and

photographed by

Bernard Wolf

Macmillan Publishing Company   New York

Collier Macmillan Publishers   London

The author wishes to give special thanks to the following people for their generous support and assistance in the preparation of this book: Judith Whipple and Cecilia Yung, Macmillan Publishing Company, New York City; Peter Wang, New York City; Liang Heng, New York City; Mao Mu Hua and Ni Ai Min, deputy section chiefs, Guilin Municipal Tourism Bureau, Guilin, Guangxi, China; Mo Jia Yun, deputy manager, Yang Shuo Hotel, Yang Shuo town, Guilin, Guangxi, China; Qin Zhen, vice director, Yang Shuo Foreign Affairs Office, Yang Shuo town; Liu Feng Lin, translator, China International Travel Service, Yang Shuo town; and finally, the Chen family of Ai Shan village, whose gracious hospitality, trust, and genuine goodwill shall not be forgotten.

The photographic prints for this book were prepared by Mike Levins.

Macmillan Publishing Company, 866 Third Avenue, New York, NY 10022
Collier Macmillan Canada, Inc.
Printed in the United States of America   First Edition

10 9 8 7 6 5 4 3 2 1

The text of this book is set in 12 point Galliard.
The illustrations are black-and-white photographs.

Library of Congress Cataloging-in-Publication Data
Wolf, Bernard. In the year of the tiger.
Summary: Text and photographs present a brief history of China and introduce the daily life of the Chen family who lives in the rural village of Ai Shan. 1. Kwangsi Chuang Autonomous Region (China)—Rural conditions—Juvenile literature. 2. Rural families—China—Kwangsi Chuang Autonomous Region—Juvenile literature. [1. China—Social life and customs. 2. Farm life—China. 3. Family life—China] I. Title.
HN740.K95W64 1988 306′.0951 87-22007 ISBN 0-02-793390-3

For Katy Takakuwa and

for Wang Youfen and

for Lee Shang Ming,

who helped make an old dream come true.

*W*ithin these massive walls there is silence for the moment. It is early morning in the Forbidden City, now a place for peace and contemplation. But once, entire armies with their horses, armor, and weapons assembled here to be reviewed by the emperors of China. Those foolish enough to gain entry to the Forbidden City without official consent were put to death, often in very cruel ways. The ancient rulers of China were not forgiving people.

Beginning in the early fifteenth century, a succession of twenty-four emperors ruled and lived here with their families, servants, retainers, chefs, artists, musicians, and concubines in opulent palaces amid wealth and luxury unimaginable to the rest of the human race. To the world, China became known as The Central Kingdom—the center of wealth, power, knowledge, and culture. Chinese inventions and art were imitated and then adapted and absorbed in other Asian cultures.

Today, any citizen of China, after paying the small entrance fee, may enter the Forbidden City and wander about. It is vast. Yet even more vast is the Imperial City within which it lies, and vaster still is the teeming capital city of China, Beijing, which encompasses these reminders of the past. But China has put her past behind her now. China is in a hurry. The oldest continuous civilization on earth is now eager to join the twentieth century. After thousands of years of political turmoil, bloodshed, natural disaster, and every vice known to humankind, life is finally, slowly, becoming better in China for most people.

An enormous portrait hangs on the gate to the Imperial City. It is of the late Chairman and Teacher of the Republic Mao Tse-Tung, the man most responsible for the recent changes, the most sweeping in Chinese history. It was he who led a ragged army of peasants to eventual victory over the Japanese invaders. It was he and his ragged army who drove a corrupt Chiang Kai-shek out of China to count his pilfered U.S. dollars on Taiwan. It was he who rid China of her warlords and ruthless land-owners. In spite of his later mistakes, many regard him almost as a god.

All too often, those who achieve absolute power lose perspective. Whatever the reason, in 1966, Mao Tse-Tung launched his "Great Proletarian Cultural Revolution," with devastating consequences for China. He called upon the discontented youth of the republic to join him in eliminating the "four olds": old ideas, old habits, old customs, old culture, and, he added, old foreign influences. With his blessing, the "Red Guards" were formed. These bands of youths, fanatically faithful to Mao's "sayings," created an atmosphere of terror wherever they roamed, brazenly attacking even Communist officials whom they considered "decadent bourgeoisie." The have-nots wanted what they could not have before and, for ten terrible years, set out to obliterate all that represented the prestige and privilege they resented. Through wanton acts of vandalism, priceless works of art, literature, and architecture were destroyed. Intellectuals, scholars, writers, poets, artists, and journalists were labeled "decadent" and savagely persecuted—some brutally beaten and thrown into prison, others killed summarily by mobs. Those with the time and means escaped into exile, forced to live out their lives in strange lands.

Diplomatic relations with many Western nations came to a grinding halt, as did foreign trade and commerce. It was a time of nightmares. Neighbor spied upon neighbor, and many were quick to rationalize old grudges when turning in the people next door. Communist youths reported their own parents for "wrong thinking": It was "the right thing to do."

When the fury had spent itself, China, bruised and shaken, discovered to its dismay that some "olds" are indispensable, even for a new nation.

There are those in and outside of China who will never forgive Mao for those terrible years, but his original vision and many of its fruits have been truly great. Under his leadership, China was transformed into an immense, restless experiment, constantly shifting course, cautiously eager to find better solutions to old problems. Some solutions worked and some didn't. At this moment, one out of every four human beings on this planet is Chinese. The experiment continues, and its course is of vital importance to the rest of us, wherever we happen to live.

Outside the Imperial City lies a world in ceaseless motion. Dusty China and a billion people! One billion and growing. Although the government is making efforts to control the size of the population, with varying degrees of success, the question remains: How are so many to be fed, clothed, housed? How transported? The only automobiles are taxis or official cars owned by the state. Trucks and vans are used to haul goods and food. There is an elaborate bus system for those who don't mind close body contact, and Beijing even boasts a new, though limited, subway. But, in China, the bicycle reigns supreme. And for those who cannot yet afford one, walking is a slower but cheaper substitute. Everywhere there are seas of restless humanity, talking, walking, laughing, munching, shopping, carrying every sort of burden—including children—on their bicycles or in their arms or on their backs. No one minds the jostling. No one grows irritable or claustrophobic. It is the way of things in an ancient land.

Now, in autumn, there is finally a respite from the summer's relentless heat, but the dust remains. When the winds blow, the dust from the northern plains is swept like a dense screen over the city, and the people must wear scarves over their faces to breathe. In spite of the staggering size of China's population, there is little unemployment, though no one grows rich. And there is housing for practically everyone at low cost. In Beijing there are mile after mile after mile of high-rise concrete blocks, each containing hundreds of tiny, unfinished, cold cubicles. No frills here, but housing nevertheless. Running water is provided, but little else. Electric power is costly and used sparingly. Each room boasts a bare light bulb suspended from a naked wire fastened to the ceiling. It is primitive housing by Western standards, but most adult Chinese can remember when such luxuries as running water and electricity were unheard of for the masses. China has undergone other changes as well: Education is available to all children at very low cost, and everyone receives medical care, paying whatever they are able! But China's greatest achievement, greater even than the Great Wall, is that there is little or no known starvation in the republic now. Without food, people die and governments are meaningless; priceless art becomes rubbish and people's noblest thoughts are forgotten. Yes, there is new hope in China today.

"Where there is water, there shall people flourish." So thought Emperor Ching Shi Huang of the Chin dynasty more than two thousand years ago. So he embarked on an astounding engineering project to divert and dam the waters of the great River Li and tame them to flow into a newly constructed canal running through the town of Shing An. The Ling Canal still functions flawlessly and to this day is the focal point of life in Shing An town. Fishermen pole their slim bamboo rafts along its surface on their way to the river. People bathe in the canal and brush their teeth here. Water is scooped up in buckets and carried home to be boiled. Farmers bring their neatly trimmed bundles of cabbage to the canal, where they carefully wash the soil from the vegetables before carrying them to market. Housewives do their laundry here while exchanging gossip. And in spite of the many abuses to which the water is subjected, it remains remarkably clean, thanks to a constant infusion of fresh water into the canal from the mouth of the dam.

Do the citizens of Shing An frequently pause to ponder this marvel? Well, as in any Chinese town, market day is market day, and business comes first. The cotton-candy man spins his magic before the fascinated eyes of eager children. In the market square it's wall-to-wall people—looking, buying, selling, ever restless and noisy. Farmers from all over this region are here with their produce and will not return home until everything is sold.

The Guangxi Autonomous Region lies fifteen hundred miles southwest of Beijing. In its countryside China weaves her timeless magic. For thousands of years, China's greatest artists and poets have attempted to capture its mysterious beauty. Here are gigantic limestone hills shrouded in mist, covered with vegetation and trees. The golden River Li and its tributaries meander around their bases. Tiny, mud-brick villages surrounded by gleaming, cultivated fields nestle between the toes of the hills. Here there is peace, away from the city's clamor. Late in the afternoon, a farmer takes his ox for a stroll and waits patiently while his beast enjoys a fresh vegetable meal at the edge of a field. Another farmer gathers vegetation from the bed of a stream to feed to his pigs.

15

And on the Li Jiang, the famed cormorant fishermen are setting out for their night's work, their slim bamboo rafts carrying fourteen to twenty passenger birds. These birds are valuable. They are trained when young, and many live to be thirty or older. By nightfall, the fishermen have arrived at the spot where they will fish. Small lanterns are lit on their rafts to attract the fish. Now the cormorants are pushed into the water to hunt. Each bird has a cord tied around its neck to prevent it from swallowing its catch. The birds dive, swim back to the rafts with their fish, then set out again for new victims. At the end of a good night's work, there will be enough to feed the families of these men. What is left will be sold in the villages. These fishermen, unique as they are, play a very small part in what is significant to China.

18

In spite of its vast bulk, only 12 percent of the republic is suitable for agriculture. The rest is craggy mountain and desert. But here, in this dreamy landscape, water is plentiful and the soil rich. In the evenings, the peasants water their small cabbage patches painstakingly, lovingly, by hand, running back and forth to the village streams for more water, their shoulder poles bending with the burden. Here lies China's greatest treasure—the land.

Yang Shuo county, in the middle of the Guangxi Autonomous Region, is an area dotted by hundreds of little villages, all looking much alike. The sizes vary a bit. Some are more prosperous than others. To the casual eye, there is little that speaks of the dramatic changes that have affected the lives of the peasants who live here. The autumn harvest has begun, and the rice is being cut, as it has been for thousands of years, by hand. At village streams and irrigation canals, women squat to scrub their laundry while exchanging friendly gossip. Old men warm their fragile bones in the early morning sun; a young neighbor offers a match for an unlit pipe. A woman joggles by, two buckets of water suspended from her shoulder pole, in that gait so peculiar to the Chinese when they carry heavy burdens: half dance, half walk, and graceful at the same time.

Another old man, determined to be of use, salvages every last grain from his son's new rice cutting as he sieves the dregs through a fine-mesh straw basket. Everywhere, the patterns of life proceed in a busy but unhurried, timeless rhythm. Those who can no longer work receive the respect befitting their age. Their advice and experience are valued. They have earned their rest. Here and there can be seen reminders of an unpleasant past: the great houses of former landlords, their ornate roofs now in need of repair, their walls stripped of their former finery. Now, some are used as schoolhouses; in others, village headmen live. Little is wasted. All is absorbed into the needs of the present. It has always been so.

For millennia, Chinese peasants have measured their wealth by the number of their sons. More sons have always meant more strong arms to work in the fields, and that has always meant more rice for the family. And despite the republic's efforts to dismantle the family as the core of Chinese loyalty, the family still comes first, always, no matter who rules in Beijing. So it has always been.

Here, no one likes to be idle. Even the very old find ways to be useful. Great-grandfathers look after their great-grandchildren while the mothers work. For these doting old men, it is a joyful occupation. Indeed, some say that they spoil their charges. But few things give more pleasure than a fat and happy child.

Throughout the land, village life is much the same as it has always been. An old man perches in concentration at the edge of a stream with a wooden pole in his hand. Is he fishing? No. He's dangling a bunch of vegetables in the water to wash them. Ancient painted scrolls depict the identical activity with uncanny likeness. And so it is with the farmer driving home his flock of ducks, using a long stick to keep them in formation.

The farmer hoeing a field today would be almost identical to another thousands of years earlier doing the same work in the same way, using a similar tool. The past fuses with the present to blur reality. If nothing has changed, then what is different now?

The People's Republic of China was established in 1949. Everyone in the republic refers to that event as "the liberation." For the vast majority, it was exactly that: a liberation from poverty and hopelessness. The short period following Mao Tse-Tung's leadership of the nation saw the most awesome changes in China's long history.

The first goals of the new republic were to restore the economy and to create workable, socialist institutions. But the most burning question was, What to do with the land? For three years following liberation, the land remained private property. Then the government declared that henceforward all the land in China would be the property of the state and its use would be determined by the state and its representatives. Reforms were introduced fairly to redistribute the land among the peasants. These were accompanied by widespread executions of landlords and rich peasants who were not friendly toward the liberation. Even those who were merely suspected of nonsympathy toward the new government were killed. When passions run high, men run mad. It would have been impossible for Beijing to have known if the victims were innocent or guilty. No doubt there were more urgent matters at hand. Having issued the directives, the government left to newly appointed legal representatives how best to administer them. So, while it is not apparent to the casual eye, life for the farmers in the villages is very different now.

The village of Ai Shan is about one thousand years old, not ancient by Chinese measure. It is home for a thousand peasants—men, women, and children—whose principal occupation is farming. The compacted earthen road flanking the village is the main artery linking Ai Shan to the rest of Yang Shuo county. Passing vehicles raise small dust storms, which are slow to subside. Within the village itself, there is one main, stone-lined street bordered by mud-brick row houses facing each other. There are no luxuries here. While most families have electricity, it is used sparingly and only at night. There are no central heating and no indoor plumbing of any kind. The village is blessed with a plentiful supply of water, but it must be fetched in buckets from the village well or from a stream or from the nearby tributary of the River Li. Toilets are holes dug in the ground in secluded spots behind the houses, between the pigs, the chickens, and the water buffalo's stall. Ai Shan is neither rich nor poor. It is not a comfortable or an exciting place to live in. But without Ai Shan and the millions of other villages like it, China could not survive.

34

The Chen family are relative newcomers to the village. They moved here from another nearby village in 1941. Mr. Chen, now forty-seven, remembers well his boyhood days. His father and mother earned a living by making and selling bean curd. Over the years, his father had put aside some money. With these savings, he decided to buy a house in Ai Shan. At that time, Ai Shan was the major market center for Yang Shuo county. The house provided shelter and little else, but he reasoned that his business would grow at this center of trade. And while, for years, the family sacrificed creature comforts, grow it did. Everyone worked hard making the bean curd, including Mr. Chen when he was not at his studies with his private tutor. Before the liberation, there were no public schools in China. Parents had to pay for their children's education. Many who could not afford it paid anyway, depriving themselves of necessities. Life was hard, and made harder by the oppressive landowners who charged exorbitant rates for the use of their land. Since they had no land to grow anything, the Chens were forced to buy all the food they needed, leaving little money for anything else. But after the liberation, Ai Shan was made part of an agricultural commune, and the land was distributed among the peasants according to each family's size and ability to use it productively. Young Mr. Chen attended the new state-run school in Yang Shuo town with all the other village children. He also joined the Ai Shan Youth Production Team and, working in the fields, refined his agricultural skills. Today he is a farmer. Now his family grows almost all the food it needs. The family has expanded, there is peace in the world, and the future holds promise.

Mr. Chen's wife, Mo Feng Yin, also forty-seven, is an energetic and warmhearted person who adores children. She has five of her own, three sons and two daughters. In China, married women retain their own family names. It is seven A.M. She has prepared breakfast for her family and seen them off to work and school; fed the pigs, the chickens, and the ox; cleaned the kitchen; swept the floors as well as the street in front of the house; completed a laundry of small clothing and hung it up to dry in the back; and taken a large load of laundry to the river to wash later. Her day is just beginning, but it is with genuine pleasure that she greets the arrival of a neighbor and her infant son.

The Chens' living room is a large, cool space with mud-brick walls and a high ceiling at the front of their house. It's a comfortable place to be in hot weather, but difficult to heat in winter. The front doors to the street are always kept wide open when there is someone at home, and no one complains when the village children wander in and out, forever curious about what's going on. As she watches her neighbor feed her child, there is a tinge of nostalgia in Mo Feng Yin's gaze. All of her children are fine young men and women now. She must wait until she becomes a grandmother. Then, once more, she may cuddle and pamper little ones to her heart's content.

But now there is work to be done. She makes courteous conversation until her guest is ready to leave. With a final sip from her glass of hot water, the woman thanks her host for the drink and carries her child home. Peasants seldom indulge in the luxury of hot tea, but in every house there is always a huge thermos of boiled water to quench thirst. Mo Feng Yin walks swiftly down the path leading to the river, with two straw panniers dangling from her shoulder pole. There is an elaborate network of earthen paths spreading out from the village center. These connect the many fields that belong to Ai Shan. They are flanked by deep irrigation troughs. Even at a close distance, the paths are not easy to see. They are so narrow that in many places there is barely room for two feet set side by side, yet the villagers dart along them as if on a broad, paved road, carrying their heavy burdens.

At the river's edge, Mo Feng Yin finds other women already at work soaking soiled clothes, rubbing them with soap powder, then soaking them again and beating the last of the soap out with wooden paddles. Surely there is no lovelier washbasin than this on earth. But the river serves another vital purpose. Because of the river, Ai Shan village is luckier than others. There is a small power station nearby that pumps water into the village irrigation ditches, carrying it to most of the fields when needed. Unless there is serious drought, the fields never go dry.

For nearly two months, Mr. Chen has been hard at work constructing a new house in the village. The work must be completed soon because his rice fields will be ready for harvesting shortly. A small man, his appearance is deceptive. Like the bamboo, his body is slender, yet supple and remarkably strong. While he likes farming, he loves to build houses, and his talents are in demand when he has the time. It was he who, fifteen years ago, undertook the complete reconstruction and enlargement of the hovel his parents purchased when he was a boy. Now, he feels, even that is inadequate. He would like to build a more comfortable home for his family, but there is not enough money for this. He has three grown sons to marry. Weddings are very expensive, but they are one of the highlights of every parent's life. The other is the birth of a grandchild or a great-grandchild. Thus is the future secured. To this end, the Chens cheerfully forgo luxury in their lives.

However, there are advantages to being a farmer. In China, all those who work for the state are required to retire at the age of fifty-five. This is done to provide new job openings for an overpopulated society. But farmers can work for as long as they like or are able to. The other advantage is in being close to the source of food. So, while he is not entirely content with his situation, Mr. Chen never complains about it. He and his wife saw starvation firsthand when he worked in a big city years ago. They are not likely to forget it.

In the afternoon, Mo Feng Yin leads the family's ox to a small cabbage patch outside the village. Here she allows the beast to graze where she can see that he is not damaging anyone's crops. Oxen and water buffalo are valuable animals. In a land where tractors are scarce, they provide the power needed to plow the soil. Mo Feng Yin spreads pig manure carefully around each tender young plant. Next, each plant must be watered individually. This is a time-consuming task, for there are no irrigation ditches to supply water to these little fields. She must run back and forth to a stream, refilling her buckets, until the job is completed.

While his parents are busy at their work, Chen Qi Xun uses this quiet time before the autumn harvest to do what he loves best, painting. In the bedroom of his still-incomplete new house, he is painting a landscape in the classical Chinese tradition, using brush and black ink on paper. When he was six, his father taught him a little of how to paint people; but surrounded by the beauty of his countryside, he found landscapes more to his liking. Now twenty and the youngest of the Chen family's sons, he longs to be an artist. He has talent, but he is self-taught, and he knows he needs training and guidance. Since graduating from middle school three years ago, he has tried twice to enter the Guangxi College for Art, but failed because he was poor in mathematics, and his Western style of oil painting was considered unacceptable. Since then he has stayed at home, painting and helping his parents at planting and harvest times. He hopes to find a good teacher, but meanwhile, an art dealer is selling his paintings in Yang Shuo town and they are selling well. If she sells a painting for thirty yuan, she gives him five yuan. One yuan equals about twenty-seven cents in U.S. currency. That may not seem very much by Western standards, but in China, one yuan, if wisely spent, can buy a meal. With an average income of one hundred yuan per month from the sale of his paintings and with the full support of his family, Chen Qi Xun is not discouraged by the obstacles to his ambition.

The morning mist softens the contours of the hills around Ai Shan. The air is rich with smells of the earth. Along paths encircling the village come the children on their way to school. They come from other nearby villages, too, for not every village has a school—some are too small to make this practical. Ai Shan has both a primary school and a kindergarten where children begin their formal education at the age of five. One of China's highest priorities is to raise the educational level of the masses. Illiteracy is becoming a thing of the past. But with each new wave of children ready for school comes the need for more new teachers, and the state cannot train them quickly enough. Sometimes, compromises must be made.

Today marks the beginning of a new career for young Li Gui Zheng, who has just graduated from middle school, the equivalent of high school in the West. She has been pressed into service as the new kindergarten teacher in Ai Shan. The teacher she is replacing has retired because of ill health. In fact, Chinese teachers are not permitted to leave their posts or change careers for other reasons, so badly are they needed. Li Gui Zheng is very nervous about her responsibilities, but the children in her class, sensing her sincerity, quickly warm to her, and the tension is eased with singing and laughter. After a while, she leads the children to the building's inner courtyard for a game of blindman's buff, which everyone enjoys.

At another building close-by, primary school classes are in progress. Here, the atmosphere is more formal as the older students carefully repeat what their teacher has written on the blackboard. The major subjects taught are Chinese, mathematics, history, music, and drawing. After completing their sixth grade here, these students will continue their education at the middle school not far from Ai Shan. But, except for those colleges that train students as teachers or in other badly needed skills, education is not entirely free in China. Parents must pay a fee for their children from the time they first attend school. The amount varies according to the class the child attends. For example, parents pay ten yuan for the kindergarten year, and more as the child progresses through primary and middle school.

There are few parents who consider this a financial burden. Since ancient times, the Chinese have prized learning almost as much as food and shelter. Ever practical, they are also aware that a good education means better opportunities in the adult world for jobs that pay more money. These are harder to obtain here than in the West because of the vast number of young people competing for them. As for teachers, even by Chinese standards, they are not very well paid. In spite of this, the majority practice their calling with enthusiasm and in the firm belief that they are helping to shape a new and better China. And so they are. For those who teach in Ai Shan, next year promises great satisfaction. The present school facilities are too cramped and inadequate, but not for much longer. For more than a year, the village has been constructing a large new schoolhouse, big enough to contain both the kindergarten and the primary school, with room to spare! It's the largest construction project in the history of Ai Shan, and everyone is excited about it.

Grandmother Mo Da Mei is sixty-one years old, but it's hard to believe. Mr. Chen's mother hasn't a gray hair on her head, and her vigor has not lessened with her years. As the matriarch of the Chen family, her counsel is highly respected, and few family matters are decided without her approval. She and her husband, seventy-one-year-old Chen Shi De, manage Ai Shan's peanut oil press, which services several villages in this part of the county.

The rough building they live in also houses three assistants plus the machinery for processing peanuts as well as the press itself. It sits at the side of the main road, easily accessible to the farmers of this area, who bring their peanuts here either to sell or to exchange for peanut oil. They use a measuring system almost as old as China itself. Everyone checks the counterweight, and when it balances with each basket of peanuts, its position on the balancing pole determines the correct weight of the basket. This farmer decides to take cash for his crop.

While Grandfather Chen pays him, Grandmother Mo empties the baskets of peanuts onto the large grain floor in front of the building. With a wooden rake, she spreads the peanuts evenly on the ground to dry in the sun. When first harvested, they retain much of the moisture from the soil in which they were grown and must be dried before their oil is extracted.

56

To her delight, her work is interrupted as a small figure runs toward her crying, "Grandmother! Grandmother!" It is Ping, her two-and-a-half-year-old great-grandson, trailed by his beaming mother. He picks up a rake and with great self-assurance begins spreading more peanuts on the ground. "Let me help you, Grandmother," he says. "I know how to do it!"

Grandmother Mo laughs approval, the gold in her teeth flashing in the sun. The child is a joy to her heart and a constant river of surprises. Where does he get his quickness? Why, even at his tender age, he can think and speak as well as many adults. But her pleasure is cut short by a loud *whump* and then total silence.

She drops the rake and runs into the end of the building that houses the equipment. There she finds her assistants gathered around the power generator, shouting excitedly. The generator has stopped working. After patient questioning, she learns that one of its parts is broken and must be replaced. Without the generator, no further work can be done. "Let me see that," says Grandfather Chen. "I think I know where I can get another one." He takes the part, runs to get his bicycle, and pedals quickly off to another village. For a while, the men pass the time reading. But they are too restless to sit quietly and decide to play a game of poker instead. Grandmother Mo looks on with interest while bluffs and challenges rage before her. The stakes are small, never more than a few fen, but it doesn't matter. Gambling is like a fever to the Chinese. When it takes hold of people, everything else is forgotten.

Two hours later, the rising tension is broken by the arrival of Grandfather Chen with a new part for the generator. The men smile with relief and hurry to fit it into the machine. No one likes being idle. Unfortunately, after the part is installed, the generator *still* doesn't work, no matter how much it's fiddled with. Now what? A mechanic must come and fix it, but the nearest mechanic is in Yang Shuo town, more than four kilometers away. Rather than make another trip, Grandfather Chen runs to Ai Shan's village office. Here is the one telephone in the entire village. It is used only for official village business or emergencies. Today, the headman's secretary is on duty. He places the call for Grandfather Chen. The mechanic will arrive as soon as he is free to leave Yang Shuo. The question is not asked when that might be. So, once more, everyone must wait. Grandfather Chen is a poor waiter, a man who is happy only when he is busy. It is with special pleasure, then, that he greets the arrival of a farmer bringing peanuts from a village eight kilometers away. It has been dry lately. Many farmers have stopped harvesting their peanuts. When the ground is dry, it is too difficult to pull the roots out of the soil. This has caused frustration for Grandfather Chen because of the drop in business at the press.

The farmer wants oil in exchange for his peanuts. After the weight of his crop has been agreed upon, Grandfather Chen leads him to where the oil is stored in large wooden casks. He ladles it carefully into plastic containers, not spilling a drop. In China, peanut oil is almost as important as rice. In a land where fuel has always been scarce, a way had to be found to cook food as quickly as possible. And so, the Chinese invented stir-frying. A small but intense fire is set under an iron wok, and a few spoonfuls of peanut oil are poured in. When the oil begins to smoke, precut, bite-size pieces of food are thrown in, together with condiments, and stirred vigorously for a few minutes with a long metal spatula. The food is scooped out and served immediately, usually with rice. This technique has given the world one of its greatest cuisines, limited only by individual inventiveness.

And now it is time to settle accounts. Grandfather Chen and his wife sit at a small, high desk in their bedroom, which also serves as an office. He makes his calculations on an abacus, the world's oldest kind of calculating machine. So much for the farmer's peanuts. So much for each container of oil. Then, beyond the break-even point, the cost of time and labor to make the oil must also be calculated. The man is selling 140 jin of peanuts in their shells. He is buying 23 jin of oil. Each jin equals one and one-third pounds. Therefore, he must pay a balance of thirty-seven and a half yuan for the oil. The farmer has listened intently to Grandfather Chen's calculations. He agrees that the figures are correct and, after careful scrutiny, hands over some badly worn yuan notes.

Late in the afternoon, the mechanic from Yang Shuo arrives and fixes the generator, but by then it doesn't make sense to start the complex cycle of making the oil.

The next morning, everyone is up before dawn, and after a quick breakfast, work begins in earnest. The assistants wear nothing but swimming trunks and sandals because of the heat and dust. In another chamber, the peanuts are passed through a roller, which separates the nuts from the shells. The nuts are carried in baskets to the main work area, where they are poured through a funnel into a grinding machine. Here, two men scoop up the ground nuts into huge sieves, shaking them vigorously to separate the meat from bits of skin and shell. The process is repeated several times, until what remains is a fine powder or flour. This is gathered and brought to a small, clay-brick oven where a man squats, stoking the flames with peanut shells, while pumping a hand bellows.

In a recess on top of the oven is a large wok. Another worker pours some of the peanut flour into it and, with his bare hands, works it around until the oil locked inside begins to seep out. The third man places a wire hoop on the ground beside the oven, into which the hot peanut flour is poured. Then, in what can only be described as a mad dance, he stomps on the flour with his feet, moving in every direction to insure that it is firmly compacted. What emerges is a peanut pancake that joins its companions near the press.

By the end of the day, there are two long rows of these, and it is time to begin the final step. The oil press has been fashioned from the hollowed trunk of a large tree. The peanut pancakes are placed into the upper part of this tunnel, and thick hardwood wedges are inserted at the end. Two men take up enormous mallets, brace themselves, and, with piercing cries, each in turn brings a mallet crashing down on the wedges. When the last wedge is in place, the day's work is finished. The peanut oil drips out, drop by precious drop, through a trench at the bottom of the press and into a container. It will be collected in the morning.

As far as anyone can recall, the autumn rice harvesting has always begun in Ai Shan around the end of October. But in other villages of the county, the harvesting is almost over. Perhaps this is because of the county's unusual terrain. Sometimes, when it is dry in Ai Shan, it may be raining in a village just the other side of the nearest hills. In any case, it is always best to cut the rice when the weather is dry. The Chens have planted a small, unirrigated field with glutinous rice, a variety that does not require flooding with water. But, as a result, rats can get at it and have begun to eat it. Rather than wait until it is fully ripe, Mo Feng Yin will spend the morning cutting the field by herself and carrying the stalks of grain back to the village. She will need to make several trips, but the day is fine and she chats with a good neighbor on the way.

When, around noon, Mr. Chen comes home for lunch, he is not surprised to find his mother busy in the kitchen. Grandmother Mo frequently cooks for the family when her daughter-in-law is occupied with other work. Her family is her world. For them, no effort is too great. She and her husband earn two thousand yuan each year from managing the peanut oil press, but they do not consider that this money belongs to them. Instead, they and all the other working members of the family put their earnings into a common pool from which each may draw according to his or her need. The plan works well, but there is rarely enough money for anything other than basics. Two thousand yuan multiplied by twenty-seven cents equals 540 dollars. Even in China, that sum cannot be stretched very far over a year's time—not for a large family of nine people.

Soon, Chen Dung Mei arrives from school for her lunch. At fourteen, she is the youngest of the Chens' children. She is followed by her brother, Chen Qi Xun; last, her mother arrives, smiling and flushed from her morning's work. After washing up, Mo Feng Yin helps Grandmother Mo finish cooking, and everyone sits in the front room to eat. The meal is a simple one, consisting mainly of vegetables and rice sprinkled generously with hot red-chili-pepper sauce. When Grandmother Mo goes to the big farmers' market in Yang Shuo town, she usually brings back with her a small piece of beef or some pork or a fresh fish, some bean curd, or, as a special treat, a fresh pig kidney. One of her dishes, a great favorite, is small balls of bean curd stuffed with minced pork and spices, then stir-fried. Curiously, while there are probably more chickens in China than there are people, chicken is considered the greatest delicacy, and it is the most expensive. The Chens raise chickens, as do all the other villagers. This guarantees them a good supply of fresh eggs, which they eat almost daily; but they eat chicken only on special, festive occasions. All in all, they eat well. And even if that were not so, they have their rice. Rice grown with the sweat of their bodies. Rice that even an emperor would praise, the like of which may not be found elsewhere in the world. It is this that sustains them.

Chen Dung Mei must be back at school no later than 2:10 P.M. She is an eighth-grade student at the Chen Guang Junior Middle School, two kilometers from Ai Shan. She makes the round trip twice daily on her bicycle. This will be a busy afternoon. After she and her classmates assemble, they are formed into ranks in the school courtyard for a period of physical exercise. "When the blood races, the mind becomes alert." Without doubt, these are serious young people who leave their playfulness somewhere else when they enter class.

At this middle stage of their school careers, they are locked into an escalating scale of pressure in which the state will demand more and more of them as they progress through higher grade levels. Never far from their awareness will be the certainty that to excel scholastically brings tangible rewards. They are in a race that only the brightest and most able can win. Those are the ones who will go on to colleges and universities and solid, respected positions in the fields of science, technology, industry, medicine, and government. All the rest, the majority, will settle for something less.

Of course, many elect to return to their villages and will be content to work in the fields with their families. Some will become petty bureaucrats, working in musty offices, forever shuffling papers. Some will find jobs in restaurants as waiters and waitresses or as cooks' assistants. Some will become chefs. Though it's hard work, in a large town or city it's not a bad way to earn a living. But some will be forced into jobs of drudgery and boredom with no escape, their senses becoming dulled as they grow bitter. One billion people! A heavy price for procreation.

In recent years, along with history, geography, Chinese, mathematics, physics, and chemistry, English has become a major middle-school subject, and great emphasis is being placed on its importance. Under Deng Xioping's enlightened leadership, there is a new bond of friendship between China and the United States. A brisk trade has sprung up between the two nations, but clearly there is a need for better communication. This is not easy; there are no two more dissimilar tongues on earth than Chinese and English. For the Chinese especially, merely shaping their mouths into the required positions of the English language is a heroic achievement, made possible only through typical Chinese persistence. Liu Lian Feng, the English teacher, spends more time on this one aspect of the language than on any other.

"If you do not make the right sound, an English-speaking person will not understand you," she explains to her class. Even here, there is a clear understanding that a good command of the English language may provide an edge in the future. China badly needs English-speaking Chinese in all areas of international concern. Everyone speaks Chinese in China. There's no special advantage in that.

Once every week, all of China's junior middle schools conduct what's called "a labor class." Chen Dung Mei's school plans to construct a new building in its compound, and for this project a great quantity of stone is needed. The students are organized into a labor brigade and sent off with shoulder poles and panniers to a nearby stone quarry. The stone faces have been laid bare by demolition. Teams of men are hard at work with crowbars and sledgehammers, breaking the rock into small pieces that the students load into their baskets and carry back to the new construction site. The load Chen Dung Mei is carrying weighs about forty kilos. She is not a strong girl, but she feels that this work will help her school, and China as well. She is glad to do it.

When school is dismissed at five P.M., she bicycles home, grateful for the chance to stretch her sore muscles. In the quiet of her room, Chen Dung Mei settles down for an hour or two of homework. She is a better-than-average student with decent, but not outstanding, grades. She thinks she would like to become a teacher. She is impressed by the respect that teachers receive, and by their knowledge as well.

Outside, although the day is coming to an end, people in the village are still busy. Small signs of change can be seen here and there. A work brigade staggers under the weight of an electrical pole that they will install to provide power for a new house. As new houses appear, so, too, do tokens of luxury. A few families actually own refrigerators. And there are at least a dozen television sets in the village. But owning one of these has its drawbacks. The children come in to watch the evening programs, spellbound. To ask them to leave would classify the owners as mean people. To allow them to stay makes it impossible to relax and enjoy this prized possession. Made wise by these examples, the rest of the villagers have decided that they can do without television in their homes.

Rush hour in Ai Shan occurs between six and seven P.M., when the main road is clogged with people coming home the four kilometers from their jobs in Yang Shuo town. This closeness is of benefit to the village. As the county seat, Yang Shuo offers a fairly wide variety of work possibilities, including in government offices and in government-operated as well as small, privately owned businesses. These last are on the increase throughout China and their growth is no longer discouraged by Beijing. The Chens' two elder sons now live and hold jobs in Yang Shuo, the older in the County Bureau, the younger as the manager of a restaurant.

But some things will not change. The great rice cycle draws near its fruitful conclusion. Because of its southern location, Ai Shan enjoys two rice crops each year. Winters are rarely severe. Ice and snow are hardly ever seen here. As a result, the earth can be tilled more frequently than in the north. The first planting is in March, the harvesting in June. The second planting is at the end of June and the harvesting at the end of October. To prepare a field for rice, the soil is plowed and planted with rape, a sort of green vegetable. Four months later, the fields are plowed again, leaving the rape in the soil as fertilizer. Meanwhile, in flooded paddies, rice seed has been planted, and soon waves of shimmering emerald dazzle the eye on all sides. When the tender rice shoots are ready, each one must be carefully uprooted by hand from the mud in which it grows and then carried to the newly plowed, fertilized, and flooded fields, where each shoot is replanted with equal care. The farmers work barefooted in mud above their ankles and well above their wrists. The labor is staggering, but no one complains. A China without rice would be unthinkable. Now, in just a few more days, Ai Shan's rice will be ready for harvest.

*T*here is a wedding in Ai Shan today! Su Qiau De is marrying Yong Ming Xiu from Bei Shan village, fifteen kilometers away. The young man has gone to fetch his bride. In the back of his father's house, a platoon of mature village men are seated at a long wooden table, hard at work. They've been at it since last night! Peeling, slicing, chopping—vegetables, pork, fish, beef, liver, tripe, kidneys, and chicken, *lots* of chicken! *Chop, chop, chop, chop*—in spite of the animated conversation, their cleavers—*chop, chop, chop*—never miss a stroke—*chop, chop, chop*. What a feast this will be!

Nearby, the chef stands poised over an enormous, steaming wok and, like the conductor of a symphony orchestra, transforms raw ingredients into inspired creations. The aroma of cooking food can be detected for a half mu in any direction. But when will the bride come? The guests have been waiting since early morning, hundreds of them.

Inside the house, the rafters have been draped with robes and garments of the finest silk from Guangzhou, gifts for the bride from the bridegroom's family. But the feasting may not begin until the bride appears. Then, a little past noon, there is a shout from outside: "The bride comes! The bride is here!"

First, members of her family carry *their* gifts for the bride into the house. These include a new sewing machine. The bride—a small figure dressed in black, her face hidden by the large black umbrella she holds—stands quietly by the path to the house. She does not speak or acknowledge any comments of those near her.

Now there is great rejoicing. As the bride is escorted into her new home, a barrage of firecrackers is set off to bring good luck to the newlyweds. And *now* the feasting begins. The first to be served are the elderly, out of respect for their years.

On each table there are a dozen or more different dishes. There are soups, stews, steamed dumplings, fried and braised pork, and vegetables. And those are only the appetizers! When these dishes are emptied, others are brought! No expense is being spared today. But where is the bridegroom? He's rushing around making sure that all the guests are being served. Once that is accomplished, he and his bride approach each table with a tray of glasses and a large bottle of mao-tai, a fiery liquor. The guests drink toasts to the happiness of the couple and place gifts of money wrapped in red paper on the tray. Hours later, the bride and groom sit numbly on the bed in the room that will be theirs from now on. It's only a brief respite. The celebrating will go on well into the night.

When the grain on the ends of the stalks turns a pale tawny gold, the rice is ready to be cut. Early in the morning, Mr. Chen wheels the family's handcart down the main road toward the fields to be harvested today. On board is their primitive threshing machine without which the work could not be done. It is October 29, and the weather is perfect: cool, sunny, and dry. At the edge of the first field, he is met by his wife and son, who help him unload the threshing machine and set it up. Around them lie the bundles of rice stalks they have already cut.

Husband, wife, and son now work as a well-coordinated team. Mo Feng Yin is the cutter. She uses a curve-bladed knife in her right hand to sever the stalk clusters just above the ground. When she has gathered a large bunch in her left hand, she lays it down and moves on to the next stand. As she cuts, Mr. Chen and their son, in turn, pick up the bundles of stalks and take them to be threshed.

The threshing machine holds a wooden drum that has metal hoops inserted all around. The drum is linked to a foot pedal. When the pedal is depressed repeatedly, the drum rotates at high speed. The grain ends of the rice stalks are held against the drum as it revolves, and the metal hoops knock off the grains of rice, which fall into the bottom of the machine. Primitive, perhaps, but effective. The rice stalks are tied into bundles and propped up into small pyramids to dry in the sun. They, too, have their use.

The Chen family has the right to use eighteen mu of land (Six mu equal one acre). Of these, only seven mu are rice fields. The rest are for vegetables, orange trees, sugarcane, flax, sweet potatoes, peanuts, and so forth. With three of his children living and working away from home, Mr. Chen no longer has the help he needs to make rice planting profitable. In the past, China used human manure extensively as a cheap and inexhaustible source of fertilizer. Now, chemical fertilizers have come into widespread use. They are clean, effective, and laborsaving. But they are also costly, and a lot must be used to grow rice. Because of this and because of the labor required, Mr. Chen thinks that next year he will devote more of his fields to money crops such as flax, peanuts, sugarcane, and fruit.

A large sheet of plastic has been placed over the threshing machine to prevent the grain from flying onto the ground as it is knocked off. When enough has accumulated on the bottom, Mo Feng Yin sorts through the grain, picking out bits of straw and discarding them. Then, with a shallow straw pannier, she scoops the rice out and pours it into a large sack, ties the end, and sets it aside.

As each section of field is cut, Mr. Chen and
his son grab the ends of the threshing machine and
drag it over the stubble to where Mo Feng Yin is
working. The threshing continues without pause.

In the afternoon, Chen Qi Xun slings two of the heavy sacks of grain over his shoulder pole and carries them back to his house, leaving his parents to work by themselves. He has family business to attend to. Because they are respected for their sense of responsibility, the Chen family have recently been appointed by their commune to be in charge of purchasing pomelos from all the farmers in their district. A pomelo bears some resemblance to a grapefruit and to Westerners may seem rather tasteless. But the Chinese love them. As the late, great premier of China, Chou En-lai, might have said, "When the inner skin of this fruit is fashioned into pockets, stuffed with delicacies, and then simmered in a clear broth, ah, *that* is a dish to be savored." It was his favorite, and he was a man whose judgment was rarely in error.

When Chen Qi Xun arrives at his house, he finds a group of farmers, their handcarts piled with the fruit, waiting patiently. He invites them inside, where they unload their fruit in separate piles.

Now begins the task of grading the pomelos according to size and weight. When this is completed, each fruit is marked with black ink.

The farmers follow everything with hawklike concentration. Chen Qi Xun is certain that his final calculations are correct, but it is in the nature of farmers to be suspicious when business is involved. This man has been keeping his own tally and it doesn't agree with the young Chen's findings. So they do it all over again. This time, the farmer admits with a rueful grin that he was in error after all. Chen Qi Xun pays him for his fruit and they shake hands politely. Then it's the next man's turn.

In the evening, a twelve-horsepower tractor, with its usual roar and clatter, pulls up to the house. The most widely used motorized vehicles in China, these tractors are mass-produced by the millions and prized because they use hardly any fuel. The rear flatbed section is unlinked from the engine and rolled into the house. On board the tractor are three of the commune's trade delegates, who have come to pick up the pomelos and transport them to buyers in the big cities. Much of this fruit will be sold in Guangzhou and much will be exported to Hong Kong, where it is in great demand. There is only one crop each year, and it is a tense time for those involved. A lot of money changes hands here. The Chens are responsible for most of it. They earn a couple of hundred yuan or so for their efforts. They are glad for the extra money, but they will not be sorry when, in a week or two, this business will be finished.

Being a headman of the village is not an easy job. Guang Zhi Xiang is a very busy man. He is one of Ai Shan's two headmen. Not only are his abilities needed here, but he and six others are headmen for the thirteen villages besides Ai Shan that form Chen Guang Commune in Yang Shuo county. He is mainly responsible for youth activities such as guiding Youth League members (fourteen- to fifteen-year-olds whose purpose is to help China). The youth accomplish this by working in the fields, helping old people, and, in general, being useful. He is also in charge of the local young militia composed of people in the eighteen-to-thirty-five age group. Then, he is responsible for helping the village schools when they have problems or need funds for new construction. The state pays two-thirds of the cost, and the villages pay the rest. This is fair, but the villagers need a voice to represent them to the state. Mr. Guang is such a voice. In addition, he is involved with improving health facilities and hygiene in the villages. He also issues marriage certificates and, this morning, puts his signature on a renewed driver's permit for a young villager who owns and drives a tractor. This man earns his living by hiring himself out to haul stone, gravel, grain, produce, and anything else that needs to be transported.

For all of this, Mr. Guang is paid a salary of 480 yuan per year. This, of course, is additional to whatever he and his family earn from farming. Does he enjoy his job? He's held this position for eight years. It appears that he may hold it for another eight if he so chooses. At each election, the villagers have voted him into office almost unanimously. And why is he so popular? He believes that it's because he's a member of the Communist Party. Because of this, the peasants believe and trust him. Indeed, he is a man who radiates quiet intelligence, competence, and responsibility. In China, it is extremely difficult to become a member of the Communist Party. Wanting it is not enough. Young people are screened at an early age for their qualities of idealism and dedication to the state, for their grasp of political history, for their willingness to sacrifice their own interests for the interests of others, and also for their leadership abilities. Even after many years of proving their worth, the slightest hint of corruption or weakness of character is enough to disqualify a potential candidate.

There will be an important meeting at the village office this morning. At nine A.M., Mr. Guang warmly greets the leader of his commune accompanied by his colleagues, the other headmen and headwomen of Chen Guang. Hot water is courteously poured for each from a huge thermos, and after some friendly conversation, the meeting gets under way. The first item is the rice harvest. Reports are coming in from around the district. Weather conditions have been good; there has been plenty of water, and it looks as if this will be an excellent year.

"I'm glad you mentioned water," says Mr. Guang, "because it reminds me that many of the irrigation channels are in poor shape. Shouldn't we correct that condition?"

"I agree," nods the commune leader. "Now is not too early to start organizing repair brigades before next spring's planting."

Everyone adds this to the list of things to be done. Then, one of the women brings up the subject of birth control. For years, China has been desperately attempting to convince its people to use contraceptives and have no more than one child per family. The state has tried almost every inducement to convince people that this matter is of vital importance to China's future. "What good is it if you have many children now who will grow up in a China where there will no longer be enough of anything for anyone? Not enough jobs, not enough housing, not enough land, and not enough food?" It's a sobering thought. In the cities, the campaign has been reasonably successful. But in the countryside, it has met with some resistance.

"There is a woman I have been talking to here in this village. She already has one child, and now she is pregnant with another. I have tried to convince her not to have any more children, but she would not hear of it. 'Look around you,' she replied. 'How many families do you see with only one son? My husband and I are young and strong. Why should we not also raise strong sons who will help us in the fields and honor us when we are old? No. I cannot agree.' "

There is silence for a moment. "This is not an easy matter," says Mr. Guang, "and we all know it. It requires thought, patience, and persistence."

"True," adds their leader. "We cannot threaten or frighten people. We can only try to educate them, and this we will do. After the harvest, I suggest we organize regular meetings for the villagers where we will invite experts to speak on this subject, answer all questions, supply contraceptives, and explain how they are used. Beyond that, we must use reason with those who object."

All present agree and the meeting ends.

Sunrise in Yang Shuo town is a lovely time. There are few people on the streets. Most of the twenty thousand inhabitants are either still asleep, just waking up, or having breakfast. The town's serenity doesn't last long, however. Especially not today. Today is farmers' market day in Yang Shuo town, and barely an hour after sunrise the marketplace is frantic with activity. Farmers from all the outlying villages arrive early, mostly on foot or bicycle, with huge loads of fresh vegetables or grain; chickens, ducks, or pigs; and just about anything else that can be eaten: mandarin oranges, peaches in season, fresh or dried pomegranates, sugarcane to munch and sooth the throat while shopping, with the dried remains spat casually into the streets.

The din is awesome. The smells, for the most part, are fascinating. But it isn't only food that's sold here. One winding street is literally decorated with every conceivable item of clothing for sale. Nothing fancy—just cheap, sturdy, everyday stuff. Stalls display gaudy bolts of cloth for the ladies, all, of course, "number one quality!" Bargain, bargain, bargain! Hardly anywhere in China is a purchase made without bargaining. Why, only a fool would obediently pay the asked-for price. Besides, what fun would there be in that? Here, a woman squats in the street over a makeshift kitchen, cooking sweet wheaten cakes. They are delicious.

On a quieter side street, a dignified old man sits patiently amid his large collection of herbal medications. Not only does he sell these to his respectful customers, but he also gives wise instruction as to their proper use. Everyone has his or her own appointed place.

Into this great, restless kettle of human endeavor comes Grandmother Mo, her nostrils aquiver, ready for civilized combat. She, too, has come on business, but, oh, how she loves this place, with its commotion and throbbing activity, always the same, yet always different! She has walked from Ai Shan carrying seventy-five kilos of dried peanut pancakes on her shoulders. These, broken up and mixed with other odds and ends, make a good, nutritious feed for pigs. They are popular with the farmers. But first things first. She stops at one of the many small food stalls scattered throughout the market for a quick breakfast of fresh rice noodles with minced pork. Refreshed, she then settles into her place, prepared to wait all day, if necessary, in order to sell everything she has brought. And she doesn't have to wait long for her first customer. The man picks up one of the disks, checks its thickness, raps his knuckles against it, and asks, "How much, Mother?" Grandmother Mo names her price. Raising his eyebrows in feigned surprise, the man grunts, "Too much," and walks away. With great aplomb, Grandmother Mo takes a seat on her merchandise. She can wait.

Sure enough, several minutes later, the same man returns. "I'll take ten kilos if you knock off seventy-five fen each," he says. "And that's my final offer." Not knowing to which *other* offer the man refers, Grandmother Mo eyes him shrewdly. Clearly, he will not return again. "Done," she agrees, and quickly weighs out the disks. It is wise to know when to give a little, especially when you are making a good profit. By midafternoon, all of her peanut pancakes have been sold and she has earned a fine total of sixty yuan. With a light heart she can now turn her attention to the pleasures of shopping for the family. Look at that carp swimming in the tank! Wouldn't that make a nice supper for tonight?

*A*fter more than a week, the rice harvesting is almost done, but not the work. All junior and senior middle schools have been officially closed for three days so that the students may help their families in the fields. There is no easy job here. Traditionally, the women have always done the cutting and the men the threshing. Why this is so is unclear; both tasks are equally fatiguing, though in different ways. But now, at least for the next day, Mo Feng Yin has the company of her daughter while cutting, and this pleases her.

While there is a special bond of affection between Mr. Chen and his youngest son, little is ever said or done between them to indicate that this is so. It is this way all over China. No one makes visible gestures of affection or love except toward babies or very young children. And yet there is much love in China.

In the afternoon, Mr. Chen's second elder son comes from Yang Shuo to lend a hand with the harvesting. His restaurant can do without him for a little while. In the evening, as the brothers work side by side, an elderly neighbor, walking his water buffalo, passes by and pauses for a short visit. "Huh," he sniffs. "you think that's hard work, do you? When *I* was a boy, I did ten times as much!"

The brothers laugh with appreciation. They
know that what he says is more than likely true,
just as they know there is no meanness in the man.

"Hey, Mr. Chen," the old man laughs. "Never
mind what I said. You have fine sons and you
should be proud of them!"

Mr. Chen thanks him warmly but makes no
other comment.

When the last of the day's grain has been gathered, the sacks are taken to Chen Qi Xun's house and hoisted onto the roof, where the grain is spread out to dry. Mo Feng Yin does this with a long-handled straw broom. Each grain of rice has stored within its hull some moisture from the stalk on which it grew. The moisture must evaporate before the grain can be stored; otherwise, the grain will rot. If the sun holds steady, the rice will be dry in two days. And in two days, the harvest is over; but one task remains. Not all of the grain hulls contain rice seed. Some, through random choice, are empty. These must be eliminated.

With their crop of grain at hand, Mr. Chen and his wife set up their grain separating machine in front of their son's house. As Mr. Chen pours grain into the top of the machine, Mo Feng Yin cranks a handle at one end. The handle turns a fan inside. At the bottom of the machine are two spouts. A basket is placed under the one on the right side. The revolving fan creates a current of air that blows the lighter, empty rice shells out of the left spout while allowing the heavier, seeded hulls to fall into the basket. As each two baskets are filled, Mr. Chen carries them to a cool, dry room in his son's house. The rice is left in the hull for better storage. When it is needed, it will be separated from the shell. Among them, the members of the family consume more than sixty baskets of rice each year. Two baskets will be given to the state as a tax for the use of the land. Some of the crop will be used as seed for the spring planting, and the rest will be sold on the free market at Yang Shuo town. The Chens will probably earn about 700 yuan from the rice they'll sell this year, and they consider that a good profit after all of their expenses. Last year they were not so lucky.

As the Chens continue their work, village neighbors pass them on the main road, trundling huge loads of rice straw on their handcarts. This is a key to how these people live: Nothing is wasted. The straw is taken to their homes and kept for the winter. Then, when there is little fresh vegetation, some of it is fed to their oxen and water buffalo and the rest is used to bed their stalls against the cold. Even the empty rice shells are not thrown away. The Chens gather these up and bring them home to feed to their pigs. Tomorrow, they will begin the task of taking up the rice straw in their own fields.

Not only the rice crop, but the flax, too, has been harvested, and throughout the village people sit in front of their houses stripping the leaf from the fiber, then draping the fiber over long poles to dry in the sun. For a while, Ai Shan takes on the look of a spring festival, but winter is near. Soon, agents for the state will come and buy the villagers' flax at good prices, better than what they get for their rice. The flax will be shipped to factories and made into linen, which these people will never see. And now, before the ground can harden with cold, begins the last phase of the great rice cycle. Everywhere men toil behind their water buffalo or oxen, ploughing the soil, turning the harvest's leavings into the ground in preparation for next spring's planting.

In the evening, Mr. Chen comes home carrying his crude wooden plow into the house. He sinks wearily to the kitchen floor, grateful to sit quietly while his wife gets dinner under way. For him, life is not why. It simply is, and he finds it good.

Daylight leaves Ai Shan slowly, as if reluctant to part from its beauty. The ages have been kind to this place. So much has changed, yet so much has remained the same.